THE VISIONS OF ZECHARIAH

AND BONUS BOOK: GOD'S TREASURE BOX

BRIAN JOHNSTON

Published by:

HAYES PRESS CHRISTIAN PUBLISHERS

The Barn, Flaxlands

Royal Wootton Bassett

Swindon, SN4 8DY

United Kingdom

www.hayespress.org

Table of Contents

CHAPTER 1: THE DIVINE PRESENCE

———

They were dark days in which Zechariah ministered to the people of God. Through the prophet's ministry, and into the midst of the discouragement of the times, God brought messages of hope to his people. This was the time when Jews were busy trying to resettle into their own land, after they had been deported to Babylon for a while. But re-establishing the service of God in accordance with the Word of God seemed, at times, like too much effort. That was when Zechariah's visions began - visions in which God spoke powerfully to him: visions full of relevance for the predicament, and the mood, the people were in. Let Zechariah share with us the first of the visions God showed him, he says:

> "I saw at night, and behold, a man was riding on a red horse, and he was standing among the myrtle trees which were in the ravine, with red, sorrel and white horses behind him. Then I said, "My lord, what are these?" And the angel who has speaking with me said to me, "I will show you what these are." And the man who was standing among the myrtle trees answered and said, "These are those whom the LORD has sent to patrol the earth."

So they answered the angel of the LORD who was standing among the myrtle trees and said, "We have patrolled the earth, and behold, all the earth is peaceful and quiet." Then the angel of the LORD said, "O LORD of hosts, how long will You have no compassion for Jerusalem and the cities of Judah, with which You have been indignant these seventy years?" The LORD answered the angel who was speaking with me with gracious words, comforting words.

"So the angel who was speaking with me said to me, "Proclaim, saying, 'Thus says the LORD of hosts, "I am exceedingly jealous for Jerusalem and Zion. But I am very angry with the nations who are at east; for while I was only a little angry, they furthered the disaster." "Therefore thus says the LORD, "I will return to Jerusalem with compassion; My house will be built in it," declares the LORD of hosts."" (Zechariah 1:8-16)

Notice the key promise there: God assures his people through the prophet, "I will return to Jerusalem...My house will be built in it". Building God's house was the project in which they were engaged. They were rebuilding the new temple on the same spot where Solomon's Temple has been destroyed by the Babylonians in the 6th century BC, some seventy years earlier. The work had its difficulties and there were discouraging times, but now came a tremendous reassurance that the house would definitely be built, for God was promising to be with them again. "I will return," he said. His presence would guarantee success in the mission as long as their hearts were right before him.

But wait a moment. It's worth pausing right there. Surely this is the most basic characteristic of God's house in any age: it's the place where God's presence is known in a special way. There were times in Bible history when God disowned or abandoned his house. When the Jews of Jesus' own generation proved by their rejection of him that their hearts were far from God, Jesus told them, "your house is left to you desolate" - meaning the temple at Jerusalem was in the process of being disowned by Gob as no longer being "his house". God's house - is - has to be - the place where his presence is known. If God's presence is no longer there then it's no longer his house.

God announced this principle early in Bible history, way back in the Bible book of beginnings, the book of Genesis. This first principle of God's house on earth is disclosed in the story of a weary traveler in Genesis Chapter 28. Imagine a lonely stretch of desert with the sun going down. It's setting on this traveler who might well have been occasionally glancing backwards. There's sin on his conscience. He's a man on the run. This is Jacob running away from the brother he's cheated. Wait! He's stopping now. It looks like he's preparing to spend the night. But what place is this? The Bible simply says:

> *"He came to a certain place and spent the night there, because the sun had set; and he took one of the stones of the place and put it under his head, and lay down in that place."* (Genesis 28:11)

It might have seemed like a kind of nondescript place that Jacob had merely stumbled across. It hardly seemed like a special place at all as Jacob settled down to sleep. But as he slept:

> *"... he had a dream in which he saw a stairway resting on the earth, with its top reaching to heaven, and the angels of God were ascending and descending on it. There above it stood the LORD."*

Notice the position of the LORD occupied in this revelation. This was a revelation of a place on earth where God's will is done as it is in heaven, a place where God rules. This, for Jacob, was a fresh revelation of God, the God who now said to him:

> *"I am the LORD ... I will give you and your descendants the land on which you are lying ... I am with you and will watch over you wherever you go, and I will bring you back to this land." (vv.12-15)*

When Jacob awoke he exclaimed:

> *"Surely the LORD is in this place, and I was not aware of it ... How awesome is this place! This is none other than the house of God; this is the gate of heaven"* (vv.16-17).

In more than a physical sense this was an awakening experience for Jacob. He realizes he's been staying in the very place on earth where God resides. Unconsciously, he had actually laid down to rest in the place where God himself rests! Jacob at once makes a vow of commitment, for he's understood this is the place where God rules. Coming to terms with all this is something Jacob himself describes as an awesome experience. "Surely the LORD is in this place, and I was not aware of it!"

This was a place where the divine presence was known and could be accessed. So, Jacob called the name of that place Bethel (meaning house of God) - previously the name had been Luz (Genesis 28:19). I guess for others it would remain Luz, for there was nothing for passers-by to see, no grand architecture and no impressive religious symbols or rituals. But for Jacob it was now more than special, and he would return to it. This was because he could say: "Surely the LORD is in this place."

And that's the reason why we've referred to Jacob's remarkable experience - because in this first ever Bible reference to "the house of God" we're given a defining feature of it which is: "the LORD is in this place." Without God's presence being located there in a special way, a place could never be God's dwelling-place. Perhaps that seems obvious but I think it's worth underlining at this stage.

And of course it brings us back to the first vision God gave to the prophet Zechariah. Our plan of study is to relate each of these visions to the building of God's house, for surely that's the relevance of these visions the means of encouragement for the people in their project of rebuilding the Jerusalem Temple, which would again be God's house on earth at that time. But our aim will be to learn the lessons of each vision, because I suggest to you they provide timeless principles which apply to God's house on earth in any age.

And that's of relevance to us, because you may remember Peter, when writing to born-again Christians in the first century, went to talk about the possibility of their *being built up as a spiritual house* (1 Peter 2:5). The apostle Paul had his sights on this too when he spoke of the local New Testament churches of God combining to become the *habitation for God in the Spirit* on this earth (Ephesians 2:20-22). What were the defining features of God's house in New Testament times? The same as they have always been, and first among them is this: that it's the place where the LORD declares that he's come to reside so that men and women can approach and serve him as he instructs them - a "habitation for God in the Spirit" indeed.

So this had to be the very first reassurance to the builders in Zechariah's day. The vision repeated the point God had made earlier in the first chapter about his willingness to return to them (v.3). That was essential for as Psalm 127:1 says: *"Unless the LORD builds the house, They labor in vain who built it."*

In fact, Zechariah's colleague, the prophet Haggai, emphasized the same point in his message given at the same time. He told the people: *"'I am with you', declares the LORD ... 'I am with you ... As for the promise which I made you when you came out of Egypt, My Spirit is abiding in your midst!"*

What an encouragement to the builders at that time! And what a reminder to us that God's house in any age is first and foremost 'the place of the Name' (see Deuteronomy 12) meaning a place divinely chosen to be what no other place could be at the same time - the place of the divine presence on earth.

CHAPTER 2: OVERCOMING OPPOSITION

———

Our plan in studying the eight visions we find early in the book of Zechariah is to relate each of the visions to the building of God's house, for surely that's the relevance of these visions - they were given at that time to the means of encouragement for the people in their project of rebuilding the Jerusalem Temple, which would once again be God's house on earth at that time. The second vision the prophet Zechariah received deals with the opposition the people were facing. The prophet says:

> "Then I raised my eyes and looked, and there were four horns. And I said to the angel who talked with me, "What are these?" So he answered me, "These are the horns that have scattered Judah, Israel, and Jerusalem." Then the Lord showed me four craftsmen. And I said, "What are these coming to do?" So he said, "These are the horns that scattered Judah, so that no one could lift up his head; but the craftsmen are coming to terrify them, to cast out the horns of the nations that lifted up their horn against the land of Judah to scatter it."
> (Zechariah 1:18-21)

Our aim is to learn the lesson of each of these visions, because I suggest to you they provide timeless principles which apply to God's house on earth in any age. So we'll not be attempting to go into the details of this vision, as to which particular nations were to be overthrown, and at what time. Instead, I would simply like to focus on the fact that the encouragement of this vision lay in that it promised the opposition which the builders were experiencing would be overcome. That would be welcome reassurance for the Israelites who, having returned from captivity in Babylon, were now facing resistance from the other nationals living close to the city of Jerusalem.

These were the enemies who didn't want the building project to succeed, but succeed it would because - through this second vision - God had just promised the builders would overcome their opposition. It's certainly a recurring feature of building for God that there's opposition to be faced, and by God's help, to be overcome.

In New Testament times, the apostles through their teaching were laying the foundation for the building of God's spiritual house on earth. Once again there was opposition to the building. This was experienced whenever the apostles' teaching encountered resistance. The writings of Paul, and the historical record of the early churches of God, give us the names of some notorious opponents, names like those of Alexander the coppersmith, and of Hymenaeus and Philetus.

The original doctrines of authentic Christianity came under attack early on. The "standard" teachings which the Lord Jesus had given to his apostles formed the body of doctrines which could very properly be called the spiritual blueprint for the building of God's house on earth. It was a spiritual house, of course, as in Peter's "living stones". But they were "living stones" arranged carefully according to God's pattern. Every building project needs its blueprint or pattern. Certainly, in the Old Testament both the Tabernacle and the Temple at Jerusalem had of God. These structures were not of human design or ingenuity. The Bible emphasizes the fact that Moses built to the God-given pattern, and commends him for doing so.

In this so-called Church Age, the same principle applies. The pattern is specified by the commands of the apostles found in the New Testament and put into practice, God's house takes shape, comprising every Christian who faithfully - like Moses - follows the God-given pattern for Christian who faithfully follows the God-given pattern for Christian service laid down in the New Testament. This, as we've said, was what was known as the apostles' teaching or simply referred to as "the Faith" - being the Faith, not just faith. It was the body of doctrine, the things people were to believe. So coming back to the matter of overcoming opposition, which is the feature of Zechariah's second vision, we find Jude saying:

> *"Beloved, while I was making every effort to write you about our common salvation, I felt the necessity to write to you appealing that you contend earnestly for the faith which was once for all handed down to the saints."* (Jude v.3)

You notice the implied opposition? The Faith, the pattern of instructions contained in the commands of the Lord Jesus through his apostles was something which had to be contended for. They were under attack by false teachers and false teachings. Perhaps that's a fairly blatant form of opposition. But there's another source of resistance to God's truth which is within our own selves - or should I say it's our former selves, sometimes referred to in Bible versions as the "old man" or "old self". To overcome this source of opposition, the apostle Paul writes in Roman 12.

> "*Therefore I urge you, brethren, by the mercies of God, to present your bodies a living and holy sacrifice, acceptable to God, which is your spiritual service of worship. And do not be conformed to this world, but be transformed by the renewing of your mind so that you may prove what the will of God is, that which is good and acceptable and perfect.*" (vv.1-2)

Self-will and worldliness are definite enemies of the Faith. They hinder its expression in our lives. Dying to our former self, and choosing God's will in preference to our own, is the way we can, by God's help, overcome this subtle foe through becoming living sacrifices. Paul's just mentioned "transformation" - what he has in mind is nothing less than a total change from the inside out, like a caterpillar to butterfly type change. The kind of change that ends up with us agreeing that God's will - and not our own will - is the thing that's good for us, and is in fact all we need. That has the effect of drawing our attention away from ourselves and towards the needs of others. For Paul continues:

> "*For just as we have many members in one body and all the members do not have the same function, so we, who are many, are one body in Christ, and individually*

members one of another. Since we have gifts ... let love be without hypocrisy...practicing hospitality ..." (Romans 14:4-6)

The result is we end up serving God and one another - according to our giftedness - and in the New Testament setting that takes us into the arena of logical, biblical churches of God forming God's house. In its Old Testament counterpart there was an altar for animal sacrifices connected with the house of God or Tabernacle in Moses' day. Multitudes of animals lost their lives on Jewish altars, but from New Testament times it's living sacrifices that God's looking for in his house.

When the living stones, of which God's house is now built, present themselves to God as living sacrifices, that's the way to overcome the opposition which stems from the will of our former self and the worldliness which so often accompanies it. It's by living under the shadow of the cross day by day - by being a living sacrifice - by re-orienting ourselves to the will of God. Not just knowing the will of God in terms of everyday guidance issues, but His will concerning serving Him with our gifts among his gathered people. That's what it means to live sacrificially - from the world, and for others - in the very place of sacrifice and worship (see Deuteronomy 12).

So, whether it's opposition from others who teach differently to the original apostolic teaching or whether it's a resistance that expresses itself through our own self-will, or whether it's worldly opinions trying to squeeze us into the world's mould, whichever it is - it's certainly a recurring feature of building for God that there's opposition to be faced, and by God's help to be overcome.

CHAPTER 3: SEPARATION

S o we now come to the third of Zechariah's vision from the
time the Jews were rebuilding the temple of God at
Jerusalem after their period of captivity in Babylon. We're trying
to identify the specific point of encouragement in each of these
visions - encouragement in each of these visions - encouragement
for them, but also for us. So let's take the third vision Zechariah
saw:

> "So I said, "Where are you going?" And he said to me,
> "To measure Jerusalem, to see what is its width and
> what is its length." And there was the angel who talked
> with me, going out; and another angel was coming out
> to meet him, who said to him, "Run, speak to this young
> man, saying: 'Jerusalem shall be inhabited as towns
> without walls, because of the multitude of men and
> livestock in it. For I,' says the Lord, 'will be a wall of fire
> all around her, and I will be the glory in her midst.'"
> (Zechariah 2:2-5)

At the beginning of the vision the young man was measuring
the city of Jerusalem. The implication was that the city was in
the future going to become a large, expansive city teeming with
people, so much so that it would spill over to boundaries and
not be able to be contained within walls. But there was the
reassurance that there would be no security risk because the Lord
himself would be a wall of fire around it. The city would still

need a wall of some kind of make a line of separation between the inside and the outside, and so to keep out everything that belonged outside.

In terms of the immediate rebuilding work which was to hand, Nehemiah was soon to come and rebuild the Jerusalem city's defensive wall, enclosing, of course, the temple as the house of God.

This is the point of principle I want to suggest this vision raises - that the proper functioning of God's house in any age - and irrespective of its size - requires a clear line of demarcation so we can be clear as to what's within God's house or kingdom, and what's outside of it. In terms of God's spiritual house in the New Testament, the apostle Paul had to command the local church of God at Corinth to "put away" from itself an immoral brother (1 Corinthians 5:13). He was expelled to the outside place, as no longer remaining in God's house - still in the Body of Christ, of course, for that comprises all believers - but removed from the fellowship and service of the house of God which found its local expression in the Church of God at Corinth.

The clear need to have a line - or wall - of separation between what's inside and what's outside of God's house is also demonstrated in Paul's second letter to Timothy. Let's begin our review of what's there with a point of general principle of Paul's argument:

> *"Now in a large house there are not only gold and silver vessels, but also vessels of wood and of earthenware, and some to honor and some to dishonor. Therefore, if anyone*

cleanses himself from these things, he will be a vessel of honor, sanctified, used to the Master, prepared for every good work." (2 Timothy 2:20-21)

Vessels are separated out here as to whether they are in the category of being honourable or that of being dishonourable. And from what we read around these verses, we find Timothy's going to have to deal with - going to have to separate out - honourable and dishonourable workers in God's spiritual house at that time. Here's how this difference in principle was applied in practice. Paul says:

"Be diligent to present yourself approved to God as a workman who does not need to be ashamed, handling accurately the word of truth ... [and he goes on to say] *Hymenaeus and Philetus, men who have gone astray from the truth saying that the resurrection has already taken place ... upset the faith of some."*

But Timothy's judgement as to who was approved and who was ashamed could never be a subjective or arbitrary one. The apostle set out for Timothy the basis for discriminating when he said:

"Nevertheless, the firm foundation of God stands, having this seal, "The Lord knows those who are His," and, "Let everyone who names the name of the Lord abstain from wickedness."

The kind of seal that existed in Bible times was a device such as a signet ring or cylinder, engraved with the owner's name or a design, kept around the neck on a cord or on the finger as a ring ... it featured a raised or recessed signature to leave its mark when impressed on wax or clay ... a seal usually served to certify a signature or authenticate a letter (Nelson's dictionary).

So a seal was the mark of genuineness. In this case we're talking about Gods seal of approval. It's God himself who makes the approved and honourable to be distinguished from the dishonourable and ashamed. Remember what we read: *"Nevertheless, the firm foundation of God stands, having this seal, "The Lord knows those who are His," and, "Let everyone who names the name of the Lord abstain from wickedness."* What is the foundation which has the double seal? The form of wording indicates a clear parallel with a dramatic Old Testament story where Korah and his company rebelled against Moses. Responding to the rebellion we read about in Numbers chapter 16:

> *"Moses ... spoke to Korah and all his company, saying, "Tomorrow morning the LORD will show who is His" ... Then the LORD spoke to Moses, saying, "Speak to the congregation, saying, 'Get back from around the dwellings of Korah, Dathan and Abiram. "Then Moses arose and went to Dathan and Abiram, with the elders of Israel following him, and he spoke to the congregation, saying, "Depart now from the tents of these wicked men, and touch nothing that belongs to them, lest you be swept away in all their sing".* (Numbers 16: 4-5, 23-26)

The match in both Old and New Testaments between those whom the Lord knows - and they being the one who must abstain from wickedness - is beyond coincidence. Some commentators on our Timothy scripture have thought that this matter of the Lord knowing those who are his refers to the Lord knowing the difference between the saved and the unsaved, but I suggest that's not where the whole context of Second Timothy chapter two leads us to. Think about it, the context in this chapter is all about conduct in the house of God as regulated by the Word of God; it's about what meets with God's approval and what doesn't.

Scanning the chapter, I suggest we're given clear examples of 'those who are his'. They are the 'faithful men' to whom Timothy was to entrust the good deposit of truth'; they were also pictured in the model soldier, athlete, and farmer and we glimpse them again as the 'approved workmen' faithfully handling the word of God; and as those corresponding to 'vessels of honour' prepared for every good work; and finally not forgetting the mention near the end of the chapter of the 'Lord's bond-servants.'

Set over against these were 'those who were in opposition' - people like Hymenaeus and Philetus: those, you remember, who had erred concerning the truth. That's the key here: the two camps are distinguished by how they handle the truth of God. But if the first seal is 'those who are his', the second seal is those who 'abstain from wickedness'. Once again failure to abstain from wickedness characterizes those throughout this chapter who 'wrangle about words'; who engage in 'worldly and empty chatter ... ungodliness'; who go 'astray from the truth...[and] upset the faith of some; who fail to 'flee from youthful lusts'; and who participate in 'foolish and ignorant speculations ... quarrels'.

Timothy is told that those bearing God's approval - on the basis of their faithful adherence to the truth of God's Word - have to 'cleanse themselves' (2 Timothy 2:21) from all who are dishonourable. This is what we mean by God's house having a wall of separation around it. Visible separation from error is required of workers who exhibit God's invisible seal of approval, and that's our principle for today.

For Zechariah's third vision was of the city of Jerusalem becoming very large, but the city still needed a wall of some kind to make a line of separation between the inside and the outside, and so to keep out everything that belonged outside. So the proper functioning of God's house in any age - and irrespective of its size - requires a clear line of demarcation making clear what's within God's house or kingdom, and what's outside of it.

CHAPTER 4: SERVICE GODWARD

━━━

The scene opens in dramatic fashion. The high priest isn't in the temple courts, but in something more reminiscent of law courts. Joshua the high priest is described by the lord as "a brand plucked from the fire." So in this case the high priest isn't a picture of the Lord Jesus, as he often is. But instead it seems like Israel as a priestly nation, as a kingdom of priests, is being represented by the high priest in this vision, or at least this part of it. The Israelites had just returned from captivity in Babylon. God had plucked them from the fire - brought them out of punishment in Babylon - and was now going to show mercy towards them and re-establish the service of God at Jerusalem in the temple that was under reconstruction.

When Satan is pictured at Joshua's accuser, we're reminded of how he's described in the book of Revelation as 'the accuser of the brethren' (Revelation 12:10). His hostility is directed against the people of God in every age. He's well named as being our Adversary. But our God is able to shut the lion's mouth! For, as the letter to the Romans asks: 'Who can lay anything to the charge of God's elect?' (Romans 8:33). God had dealt with his priestly people in the fire of the Babylonian captivity, so who was Satan to continue accusing them? There's no grounds for despair. The words of the hymn come to mind:

When Satan tempts me to despair;

Upward I look and see Him there

Who made an end of all my sins.

It's the Lord Jesus who's being viewed there as our defender, of course. So the Lord ordered Joshua's filthy clothes to be replaced by festal robes. But before he's clothed with priestly clothes again, the prophet utters a passionate prayer: 'let them put a clean turban on his head!' As I think of Zechariah calling out in the midsts of the vision, we get the sense of how real it was to him. I'm reminded of those who call out in their sleep when their dreams vivid. And I really find it most interesting that Zechariah steps inside the vision - as it were - with his concern focused on the high priest's headgear, the mitre or turban.

But why should Zechariah be so focused on the turban - why was he so keen to be reassured the mitre wouldn't be omitted? Some people just think it was that he wanted complete reassurance of the restoration of the priestly nation at that time, and so he naturally looked to the item of clothing that completed the high priest's wardrobe. Maybe that was part of it, but I think there's more of it. There's something connected with the turban which we can read about in the book of Exodus where Moses was commanded:

> "You shall also make a plate of pure gold and shall engrave on it, like the engravings of a seal, 'Holy to the LORD.' You shall fasten it on a blue cord, and it shall be on the turban, it shall be on the front of the turban. So it shall be on Aaron's forehead, that Aaron may bear the iniquity of the holy things which the children of

Israel hallow in all their holy gifts; and it shall always be on his forehead, that they may be accepted before the LORD." (Exodus 28:36-38)

I believe that's why this matter of the turban or mitre was so important to Zechariah, and was on his mind. He knew only too well the failings of his people. How could they ever function in the presence of God, how could they approach to the holy God of heaven in his earthly residence if there was any possibility that the inevitable imperfections of their offerings might render them less than acceptable before God? How thankful we, too, are that we have in our Lord Jesus a high priest who, Hebrews 2 says:

"... had to be made like His brethren in all things, so that He might become a merciful and faithful high priest in things pertaining to God, to make propitiation for the sins of the people. For since He Himself was tempted in that which He has suffered, He is able to come to the aid of those who are tempted." (Heb 2:17,18)

Again the hymn-writer says of our Lord Jesus, the ultimate high priest:

For us He wears the mitre;

Where holiness shines bright.

For us His robes are whiter

Than heaven's unsullied light.

How often we too, like Zechariah, need to make that our appeal! But we must pass on to other interesting things in this vision. Remember the Lord's words to Joshua in the vision?

"And the angel of the LORD admonished Joshua, saying, "Thus says the LORD of hosts, 'If you will walk in My ways and if you will perform My service, then you will also govern My house and also have charge of My courts, and I will grant you free access among these who are standing here." (Zechariah 3:6,7)

It's that last promise particularly that grabbed me. Joshua's friends were sitting before him, so I think these standing ones were angels. I wonder then if this is a reminder that God's house on earth is the gate of heaven, as in its first revelation to Jacob in Genesis chapter 28 in terms of a ladder set up on the earth with angels ascending and descending upon it?

The house of God on earth with its sanctuary is the place where the people of God have access in a special way to the immediate presence of God. But the promise to Joshua seems to carry us forward in time - as confirmed by later parts of the vision. Joshua and his friends sitting before him are symbolic. The vision isn't just about the restoration of the service of God's house in the sixth century BC, but symbolises the good times which were to come for God's house after Christ's Advent,

CHAPTER 5: A WITNESS TO MEN

―――――

A re you engaged in some difficult work for the Lord? Or maybe you regard your work as just a small work, but a work made difficult nonetheless by the attitudes of others who are involved? I remember a time when I was wrestling with church difficulties. I tumbled out of bed one morning into prayer and then from prayer to my Bible reading. My planned reading for the day was Zechariah chapter 4, our current study. It was a real encouragement to me, I tell you, to read about a man wakened from sleep to catch a vision of a golden lampstand, the New Testament symbol for a church of God (Revelation 2 and 3). Sometimes we might be tempted to see the local church where we're working as full of problems, making the work of building there for God ever so difficult, but then God gives us a different view: he shows us what it means to him. But enough, let's read more from Zechariah the prophet:

> "Now the angel who talked with me came back and wakened me, as a man who is wakened out of his sleep. And he said to me, "What do you see?" So I said, "I am looking, and there is a lampstand of solid gold with a bowl on top of it, and on the stand seven lamps with seven pipes to the seven lamps. Two olive trees are by it, one at the right of the bowl and the other at its left."

So I answered and spoke to the angel who talked with me, saying, "What are these, my lord?" Then the angel who talked with me answered and said to me, "Do you not know what these are?" And I said, "No, my lord." So he answered and said to me: "This is the word of the Lord to Zerubbabel: 'Not by might nor by power, but by My Spirit,' Says the Lord of hosts. 'Who are you, O great mountain? Before Zerubbabel you shall become a plain! And he shall bring forth the capstone With shouts of "Grace, grace to it!"'

"Moreover the word of the Lord came to me, saying: "The hands of Zerubbabel Have laid the foundation of this temple; His hands shall also finish it. Then you will know that the Lord of hosts has sent Me to you. For who has despised the day of small things? For these seven rejoice to see the plumb line in the hand of Zerubbabel. They are the eyes of the Lord, Which scan to and fro throughout the whole earth." Then I answered and said to him, "What are these two olive trees - at the right of the lampstand and at its left?"

And I further answered and said to him, "What are these two olive branches that drip into the receptacles of the two gold pipes from which the golden oil drains?" Then he answered me and said, "Do you not know what these are?" And I said, "No, my lord." Then he said, "These are the two anointed ones who are standing by the Lord of the whole earth." (Zechariah 4:1-14)

Remember the historical background to this - and the other visions? The Israelites have returned from captivity in Babylon - returned to rebuild the Jerusalem Temple which the Babylonian king had destroyed. The work was slow, there was opposition, and the emerging new temple seemed but a pale reflection of past glories. This was the cue for Zechariah's fifth vision which we've just read.

The most important feature of his vision was the encouragement it gave that the work in hand would be successfully completed through the working of the Spirit of God. Zerubbabel, the governor, had not only begun the work, he was going to finish it as well. Just as the foundation stone had been laid by his hands, so also would the stone at the head of the corner which crowned the work.

The hands of the builders had been weekends by discouragement. The older folks with long memories could remember the magnificence of the Temple Solomon had built, the one the Babylonians destroyed. The current rebuilding project seemed small and insignificant by comparison. The expression 'the day of small things' seemed to have been a disparaging term applied to the current efforts by those who longed after past glories. But while they looked back, God was looking forward. He speaks of how his eye anticipated Zerubbabel's final checks using a plumb line - the plumb-line showing the building as being true to God's own pattern. That was a source of gladness for God and he said so - how encouraging that must have been for the disheartened workers! It's worth pausing to apply that encouragement to any discouraging situation we may be experiencing in church life.

Our efforts can seem so feeble, and results may be small, but when once we have the assurance of the Spirit's working we can take heart from God's different perspective as we build the God's own pattern. So the promise was that the difficulties would dissolve away, and with an ascription of blessing, the work would be finished.

Encouragement through a dependence of the Spirit's working was obviously the main point of the vision, but a really striking feature of it is the way the prophet Zechariah was kept waiting in suspense, waiting for the answer to his question - the question he'd asked about the two olive trees. I'm sure we can relate to the business of being kept waiting. We may often read something in the Bible the meaning of which is not very clear to us, so we pray asking for help to understand it so we might apply it correctly to our lives. But it seems as if it's some time later before - by some means or other - we get the help we've asked for.

Well, Zechariah knew here what it was like to be kept waiting. Early on in the vision, when his attention was drawn to the olive trees on either side, he asked the question 'what are these?' The immediate answer he received was not specifically about the olive trees as such however, but instead gave the prophet - and us - the key to interpreting the whole vision. Which we say again, was to make abundantly clear that in any work for God it's the Spirit of God who produces the results. We should labour as if it all depended on us, but we should never believe for a minute that it really does: it's not by a human might or power, but by the Holy Spirit's working that God's work is done. That's why in this vision there's no representation of anyone pressing the olives, but only of channels through which the oil flows to give the light of witness. It's like the old hymn says:

Channels only, blessed Master,

But with all Thy wondrous power

Flowing through us

Thou canst use us

Every day and every hour.

Near the end of the vision Zechariah again enquires about the two olive trees, and in his eagerness even repeats the question. Finally, the long-awaited answer is given; but not before the angel has expressed surprise that the prophet didn't know. At last the build-up is over and the answer comes: *"These are the two anointed ones who are standing by the Lord of the whole earth."* (v.14)

Perhaps it seems like an anticlimax! After all, that we might have wished the answer was plainer to understand! However we venture to suggest that since this chapter has featured the work of Zerubbabel, and the previous chapter focused on the office of Joshua, these two are likely the ones being referred to in the first instance. Zerubbabel belonged to the line of the kings, and Joshua was high priest. Since both kings and priests were anointed, then maybe these two named individuals - individuals intimately involved with the work of rebuilding - are the most likely candidate for being the 'two anointed ones.' Perhaps the way is already being prepared for the recognition of the Messiah in a later chapter, one who will combine both offices and sit as priest of his throne.

Let's emphasize the timeless lesson of this vision: that the house of God on earth is designed to be a witness to the truth of God. To that end it functions by the Spirit of God with God-given light. In the book of Revelation, the witness of local churches of God (chapters 2 & 3, as well as the witness of individual prophets (chapter 11), is described in terms of them being lampstands). The overall significance of the use of the term 'lampstand' in our Bibles seems to be the idea of Spirit-given light for witness - for bearing testimony before men and women.

CHAPTER 6: WHERE GOD'S WORLD RULES

———

I think it was in Belgium where I first noticed them. Huge flying adverts. They were towed behind small aircraft over densely populated areas. You'll understand why that comes to mind as we come now to vision number six from Zechariah:

> *"Then I turned and raised my eyes, and saw there a flying scroll. And he said to me, "What do you see?" So I answered, "I see a flying scroll. Its length is twenty cubits and its width ten cubits." Then he said to me, "This is the curse that goes out over the face of the whole earth: 'Every thief shall be expelled,' according to this side of the scroll; and, 'Every perjurer shall be expelled,' according to that side of it." "I will send out the curse," says the Lord of hosts; "It shall enter the house of the thief and the house of the one who swears falsely by My name. It shall remain in the midst of his house and consume it, with its timber and stones."* (Zechariah 4:1-4)

A flying scroll, more like a flying billboard! Did you get the size? Something like thirty feet by fifteen or ten metres by five. Just as in the case of the advertisers, I think it's clear that God wanted his people to get the message all right. But as well as being big, there was another eye-catching feature: it was written on both sides. Now does that trigger any memories? A flashback to the time of Moses and the giving of the Law perhaps? Here's what Exodus 32:15-16 says:

> *"... Moses turned and went down from the mountain with the two tablets of the testimony in his hand, tablets which were written on both sides; they were written on one side and the other. The tablets were God's work, and the writing was God's writing engraved on the tablets. So it's as if this flying scroll is meant to remind us of the stone tablets written with the Word of God in terms of the Ten Commandments, written on one side and the other."* (Exodus 32:15)

There's another connection between the scroll in this vision and the stone tables containing the Ten Commandments. For the curse pronounced judgement on those who swore falsely in the LORD's name and against thieves who stole - that is, it's related directly to the third and eighth of the Ten Commandments respectively. Remember those two commands stated: *"You shall not take the name of the LORD your God in vain for the LORD will not leave him unpunished who takes His name in vain,"* and *"You shall not steal"* (Exodus 20:7,15).

In Zechariah's vision it seems as if thieves are mentioned specifically as sinners against the second table of the Ten Commandments which deals with sins people commit against each other; whereas false swearing was a sin primarily against God which is the category dealt with in the first table of the Law. So both aspects are included: things honourable in the sight of

God and men. Swearing in the name of the LORD for deceit might refer to perjury in the broadest sense of the word, or to any abuse of the name of God for false, deceitful swearing.

I think we can agree there's a definite link between this scroll Zechariah sees and the Word of God as it was given through Moses. Nowadays God's Word, the Bible, is lightly regarded by many people. But as the flying scroll graphically as the flying scroll graphically demonstrated then, God wanted the people to have a high view of his Word! - and he still does! We read in the Psalms (138:2), after all, that he has exalted his Word and his Name above all things.

In the days when God's house is no longer a physical structure, but is now a spiritual house, God's standard, of course, is still as high. The apostle Paul, in fact, brings the same two points about not stealing and not speaking wrongly into focus when writing to some of those within God's house in the church of God at Ephesus (in Chapter 4:28,29):

> *"Let him who stole steal no longer, but rather let him labor, working with his hands what is good, that he may have something to give him who has need. Let no unwholesome word proceed from your mouth, but only such a word as is good for edification according to the need of the moment, that it may give grace to those who hear."*

But let's go back now to what Zechariah saw: the huge flying scroll. Remember the size? Twenty cubits by ten. Does that ring any bells? Seem familiar? Well, it's the exact size of the first compartment - or holy place - of the tabernacle, God's house on earth in the days of Moses. And thirty feet by fifteen - which is what this amounts to - are also the dimensions of the temple porch in Solomon's temple (1 Kings 6:3). Interesting because that was where the law was usually read.

Having picked up on those two links: first the Word of God, and then the house of God, I simply want to make the point that the standards of God's house are the standards of God's Word. Behaviour within God's by the Word of God. With the physical structures we've referred to such as the Tabernacle and Solomon's Temple, it was God's Word in terms of the Law of Moses; in the spiritual house from New Testament times it's the teaching of the apostles found written as New Testament commands. Before we come to an example of those commands, let's also take the next vision Zechariah saw, for the Seventh vision is so closely related to the sixth that we'll take them together:

> "Then the angel who talked with me came out and said to me, "Lift your eyes now, and see what this is that goes forth." So I asked, "What is it?" And he said, "It is a basket that is going forth." He also said, "This is their resemblance throughout the earth: Here is a lead disc lifted up, and this is a woman sitting inside the basket"; then he said, "This is Wickedness!" And he thrust her down into the basket, and threw the lead cover over its mouth.

Then I raised my eyes and looked, and there were two
women, coming with the wind in their wings; for they
had wings like the wings of a stork, and they lifted up
the basket between earth and heaven. So I said to the
angel who talked with me, "Where are they carrying the
basket?" And he said to me, "To build a house for it in
the land of Shinar; when it is ready, the basket will be
set there on its base." (Zechariah 5:5-11)

Remember when Zechariah asked: "What is it?" He was told:
"*This is the ephah going forth ...This is their appearance in all the*
land." I suggest that links us back to the previous vision of the
flying scroll. It's the wicked Jews - those who steal and those
who swear - who have the appearance of the ephah. This was
the ordinary measure of grain, presumably in some standard
container of the appropriate volume. As the grain is collected
together into a measure in a basket so the wicked were to be
gathered out of the land. And symbolically the wings of these
great migratory birds would migrate them to Babylon.

Many interesting things flow from this, linking in with New
Testament prophecy from the book of the Revelation, and
telling how, in the end-time scenario, wickedness will again come
to its zenith in a resurgent city of Babylon - upon which the
judgment of God will fall. But staying with our chosen theme for
this study - in which we're trying to identify general principles
or conditions relating to God's house on earth in any age when
people are attempting to build a God, let's refresh our memory
from First Corinthians chapter 5 where the expulsion of an

immoral brother from the Church of God at Corinth is described. Paul says in the very last verse of Chapter 5: "… remove the wicked man from among yourselves …" (v.13).

Wicked behavior in departing from the teaching of the Word of God must never be tolerated within God's house. Just as the wicked were removed from the land in Zechariah's twin visions; so the wicked man at Corinth was removed from God's New Testament house on earth. In the New Testament, it's Peter who specifically refers to the New Testament churches overall being a "spiritual house" (1 Peter 2:5). It's no coincidence that it's he who earlier makes the point that Christians are to be holy even as God is holy (1 Peter 1:16), and later emphasizes the point by saying "judgment begins at the house of God" (1 Peter 4:17). That's the timeless point of application we've seen illustrated in this twinned vision from Zechariah chapter 5.

CHAPTER 7: WHERE JUDGMENT BEGINS

We now come to the last of Zechariah's vision for builders in God's house. It's a vision heavily accented with judgment. It also links closely with previous topic, in which we were learning the timeless lesson that behaviour within God's house in any age must be regulated by the Word of God. Wicked behaviour in departing from the teaching of the Word of God must never be tolerated within God's house. We reminded ourselves that in the New Testament it's Peter who specifically refers to the New testament churches overall as being a "spiritual house" (1 Peter 2:5), and it's Peter, too, who writes:

> *"For it is time for judgment to begin with the household of God; and if it begins with us first, what will be the outcome for those who do not obey the gospel of God?"* (1 Peter 4:17)

This sets the scene for the eighth and final vision that was given to Zechariah. The prophet was given these visions at a time when the people were resettling in the land of Israel after a period of deportation in Babylon. Actually, they had been taken there as God's judgment upon them - or their fathers at least. Now that a proportion of the people had returned for a fresh start, they needed to learn the lessons of the past. Judgment might not seem like an encouraging topic, but all these visions were given to encourage the builders in their rebuilding project so that the temple or house for God at Jerusalem might be rebuilt. Here then is Zechariah's last vision as recorded in God's Word, in chapter 6 of Zechariah the prophet:

"Now I lifted up my eyes again and looked, and behold, four chariots were coming forth from between the two mountains; and the mountains were bronze mountains. With the first chariot were red horses, with the second chariot black horses, with the third chariot white horses, and with the fourth chariot strong dappled horses. Then I spoke and said to the angel who was speaking with me, "What are these, my lord?" The angel replied to me, "These are the fourth spirits of heaven, going forth after standing before the Lord of all the earth, with one of which the black horses are going forth to the north country; and the white ones go forth after them, while the dappled ones go forth to the south country. "When the strong ones went out, they were eager to go to patrol the earth. "And He said, "Go, patrol the earth." So they patrolled the earth. Then He cried out to me and spoke to me saying, "See, those who are going to the land of the north have appeased My wrath in the land of the north."
(Zechariah 6:1-8).

The four patrols are pictured as coming from between mountains of bronze or copper, obviously symbolic - but of what? It's common to associate bronze or copper in its biblical usage with the idea of judgment. The metal's ability to withstand fierce heat led to it being specified as a covering material for the great copper altar that stood in the courtyard of God's house. There, in the place overlaid with copper, the fire of judgment consumed the sacrifices that were for sin. Judgment is clearly the theme connected with the bronze mountains here, for the patrol which headed northwards appeased God's wrath in the land of the north, which was Babylonia. It might seem then this has little to do with God's house as such, as these patrols went out from it to carry out judgments. But isn't that exactly the point Peter makes? Remember he says: *"For it is time for judgment to begin with the household of God; and if it begins with us first, what will be the outcome for those who do not obey the gospel of God?"* (1 Peter 4:17).

What we're mainly concerned with here is the starting point for that judgment - which is the house of God. God's judgment works outward from his house. Our concern then is church discipline. One place where the apostle Paul emphasizes our need to obey God's authoritative Word is in Second Thessalonians 3. Notice the number of times he uses words like "command" and "obey" as we read from verse 4 to verse 14:

> *"We have confidence in the Lord concerning you, that you are doing and will continue to do what we command ... Now we command you, brethren, in the name of our Lord Jesus Christ, that you keep away from every brother who leads an unruly life and not according to the tradition which you received from us. For you yourselves know how you ought to follow our example, because we did not act in an undisciplined manner among you...For even when we were with you, we used to give you this order: if anyone is not willing to work, then he is not to eat, either. For we hear that some among you are leading an undisciplined life, doing no work at all, but acting like busybodies. Now such persons we command and exhort in the Lord Jesus Christ to work in quiet fashion and eat their own bread...If*

anyone does not obey our instruction in this letter, take special note of that person and do not associate him, so that he will be put to shame."

This chapter begins by reminding us that the traditional apostolic teaching of the New Testament is nothing short of being the Lord's message. If we love the Lord, we'll keep his commands; and if we're steadfast then we'll hold fast to the whole of the apostolic tradition we've received in the New Testament revelation.

Dare we be selective in our obedience? That wouldn't really be obedience at all! For do we have similar authority to the apostles in order to select between what's a fundamental truth and what's a secondary doctrine? What part of the apostolic pattern found in our bibles do we have the right to dispense with? This was obviously a live issue already in Paul's day. Because he goes on to say: "*Keep away from every brother who...does not live according to the (apostolic) teaching.*" So it seems some were intent on ignoring what they didn't like. Perhaps one specific issue for some at Thessalonica was a refusal to work (2 Thessalonians 3:6, 8;1 Thessalonians. 4:11), but if that's included as important, what will we exclude as unimportant?

It's perfectly obvious from this that obedience to the Lord within his house demands separation to the apostolic commands as communicated by the preaching of Paul, remembering the assurance given in the chapter that this is in fact the Lord's own message. When disobedience to the Lord's message has to be acted upon by a separation between the faithful and the unfaithful, we're into the whole subject of discipline in the local church, such as we see illustrated throughout the New Testament Churches of God. It's not a popular or fashionable subject, but in the logical flow of Paul's teaching here this is where we go to. Church discipline is needed when the Christian standard is defiantly refused. Judgment must indeed begin at the house of God.

In his pastoral letters, but especially here in 2 Thessalonians 3, the apostle Paul spells out the form that discipline should take. He commands them to 'admonish the unruly' (1 Thessalonians .5:14): in other words, giving a first admonition. Then he says 'keep away' (2 Thessalonians 3:6): that being a measure of social ostracism if the admonition isn't heeded. 'Take special note' (2 Thessalonians 3:14), he says: in what sounds like a public censure. Then comes the instruction 'not to associate with' (2 Thessalonians 3:14) those who are disobedient: which must mean avoiding free and familiar fellowship with those who are unfaithful (v.15). Finally, and solemnly, he writes that they have to 'reject' (Titus 3:10) them: this amounts to excommunication as shown in 1 Corinthians 5, or when a brother is to be 'refused' after a second admonition a brother is to be refused.

I wonder if the practice of church discipline today has generally fallen into a measure of disuse? If so, the apostles were clearly of a different opinion. Paul spelt out the procedure step by step, even if it does make solemn reading. Of course no-one likes it, but the logic of 2 Thessalonians 3 is clear: if there's to be faithfulness to the pattern God has given - and as followed by those whom he recognizes as forming his house - then we have a corporate responsibility (1 Thessalonians 5:12-14) to carry out discipline, one in which church leaders take the initiative. Its character and tone, of course, is to be nothing other than friendly and fraternal, for it's always aiming at home re-constructive - to the goal of 'winning our brother'.

Well, maybe we've encircled the mountains of bronze long enough! In concluding this short study majoring on the essential ingredients of house building for God, let's remind ourselves we've encountered not only visions of judgment and the supremacy of the Word of God, but also vision of service before God and men, and above all the reminder that God's house is where his presence is specially known.

CHAPTER 1: A WORSHIPPING HEART

M y young daughter, Anna, has a simple plastic toy she really treasures. It's a model of a mobile home; a camper van. Its roof and one of its sides unfold to allow easy access to all the detailed features inside like seats and table. Because it opens and closes like this, Anna treats it like a storage box, and into it she places some of her best-loved toy figures and animals. We're amazed at how long she's kept this simple toy, and at how much enjoyment she's had from it. Of course, she ignores it for a while when new toys arrive on the scene, but it's the one toy above all others that she keeps going back to time and time again. Part of the secret of why Anna is so attached to it may be the fact it acts like a kind of treasure box for her small favourite playthings and any other small objects she values.

If we were to imagine God having a treasure box, I wonder what would be in it? In this booklet I'd like to make a few suggestions and invite you to check out the biblical support for each of them. We're going to try to identify from the Bible the kind of heart God treasures. Our search begins in the unlikely setting of a well in Samaria.

> "[Jesus] came to a city of Samaria, called Sychar, near the parcel of ground that Jacob gave to his son Joseph; and Jacob's well was there. Jesus therefore, being wearied from His journey, was sitting thus by the well. It was

about the sixth hour. There came a woman of Samaria to draw water. Jesus said to her, "Give Me a drink." For His disciples had gone away into the city to buy food. The Samaritan woman therefore said to Him, "How is it that You, being a Jew, ask me for a drink since lam a Samaritan woman?" (For Jews have no dealings with Samaritans.)

Jesus answered and said to her, "If you knew the gift of God, and who it is who says to you, 'Give Me a drink, 'you would have asked Him, and He would have given you living water." She said to Him, "Sir, you have nothing to draw with and the well is deep; where then do you get that living water? You are not greater than our father Jacob, are you, who gave us the well, and drank of it himself, and his sons, and his cattle?"

Jesus answered and said to her, "Everyone who drinks of this water shall thirst again; but whoever drinks of the water that I shall give him shall never thirst; but the water that I shall give him shall become in him a well of water springing up to eternal life."

The woman said to Him, "Sir, give me this water, so I will not be thirsty, nor come all the way here to draw." He said to her, "Go, call your husband, and come here." The woman answered and said, "I have no husband." Jesus said to her, "You have well said, 'I have no husband'; for you have had five husbands, and the one whom you now have is not your husband; this you have said truly."

> *The woman said to Him, "Sir, I perceive that You are a*
> *prophet. Our fathers worshiped in this mountain, and*
> *you people say that in Jerusalem is the place where men*
> *ought to worship." Jesus said to her, "Woman, believe*
> *Me, an hour is coming when neither in this mountain,*
> *nor in Jerusalem, shall you worship the Father. You*
> *worship that which you do not know; we worship that*
> *which we know, for salvation is from the Jews. But an*
> *hour is coming, and now is, when the true worshipers*
> *shall worship the Father in spirit and truth; for such*
> *people the Father seeks to be His worshipers. God is*
> *spirit, and those who worship Him must worship in*
> *spirit and truth."* (John 4:5-24)

It's amazing to think of the Lord of all grace pursuing the worship of this woman of questionable reputation! It was a time when Jews had no dealings with Samaritans; and a time when Jewish Rabbis (or teachers) tended to avoid discussions with women. And this woman may have been one that even her own townsfolk tried to avoid, but Jesus seems to have gone out of his way to meet this Samaritan woman so that he could have this conversation with her. And of all things to talk with her about the worship of God! We might have expected the Lord to talk about worship with Nicodemus, the high churchman of his day - but no, these profound truths about worship are shared with this hurting woman, someone who wasn't a Jew, and something of an outcast at that.

Jesus revealed to her that God the Father is searching for true worshippers, in other words people who worship the Father in spirit and in truth. It's here I suggest we discover that the heart that worships the Father in spirit and truth is something God really treasures - it's something he looks for and longs for, and it's precious to him.

Since this is something the Father values - something he might put in his treasure-box if you care to imagine it that way - then it's worth exploring what it might mean. Let's examine what this kind of worshipping heart is like. It's significant that the Father is singled out here - the Father is seeking worshippers. Perhaps that seems to indicate worship that's specially directed to the Father. Of course, the Lord Jesus himself can very appropriately be worshipped. In the Gospels we find people worshipping the Lord Jesus, like the blind man Jesus healed in John chapter nine.

There are, in fact, three main words used for 'worship' in the New Testament. One is concerned with a God-fearing attitude of mind; another is descriptive of bowing down; while the third emphasizes the actions by means of which our worship is expressed. This last idea seems to be the high watermark of worship as presented in the Bible. It was this kind of serving God with our actions that the Lord Jesus spoke about when he replied to Satan's temptation by saying: *"... to him, "It is written, 'You shall worship the Lord your God and serve Him only.'"* (Luke 4:8)

Notice that: 'serve Him [the Father] only'. We never read in the Bible of this particular (word for) worship being directed to anyone but God the Father. But it is used to describe the collective service or worship of the people of God in Romans chapter 9, verse 4. And the collective worship of God's New Testament people is the theme of the Bible letter to the Hebrews. The Hebrews' letter explains why the worship of God's people is to be addressed to the God and Father of the Lord Jesus - as when Peter writes: *'Blessed be the God and Father of our Lord Jesus Christ'* (1 Peter 1:3; Cp. Ephesians 1:3). It's because the people of God draw near to God through the ministry of the Lord Jesus in his office as High Priest. The Lord Jesus takes the spiritual sacrifices of God's worshipping people (1 Peter 2:5) and presents them to his Father (Hebrews 8:3). They're not directed to the Lord Jesus, but through him to the Father - the Father who longs for the worship of his people.

It's really impressive how the letter to the Hebrews keeps drawing on Old Testament picture language to make its points. The Holy Spirit is making it very clear in our Bibles that the worship of God's people today is the spiritual answer to all that happened in Jewish worship long ago - with its animal sacrifices, physically impressive robes, and as centred on a material temple known as God's house on earth.

Imagine someone walking towards you with the sun behind them. You first encounter their shadow as it projects out in front of them, then you meet the person belonging to the shadow. The Bible itself describes these Old Testament rituals as 'shadows' that were cast ahead of the coming of Christ. Jesus Christ, God's Son is the substance. We meet him personally in the New Testament, and the reality of Christian worship contrasts with the shadows of the Old Testament.

Now, in place of the material accessories and the mere shadows of Old Testament worship, the Father treasures the heart that will worship him in spirit and in truth. 'In spirit and in truth' means worship that's spiritual unlike the material worship of the

Old Testament; and the fact that it's to be 'in truth' emphasizes that this is worship that's the genuine article, the real substance, contrasting with the mere shadows of former times. Long before our heart ever seeks to worship God the Father, his heart has been searching for our worship - just like the Lord searched out the woman by the well. Yes, a worshipping heart is something he truly treasure.

CHAPTER 2: A HUMBLE HEART

———

Do you have a treasure box? Some people have safe deposit boxes where they keep their jewellery and other valuables. Maybe you don't, but perhaps you have a fire-proof box-file for important documents. Other things people keep safe are not necessarily valuable in terms of money, but hold a lot of sentimental value. If we were to imagine God having a treasure box, I wonder what would be in it? In this booklet I'd like to make a few suggestions and invite you to check out the biblical support for each of them. We're going to try to identify from the Bible the kind of heart God treasures. Through the Old Testament prophet, Isaiah, God makes a very clear statement when he says: *"This is the one I esteem: he who is humble and contrite in spirit, and trembles at my word"* (Isaiah 66:2 NIV)

The heart, or spirit, that's humble is one that God treasures. A person who has a humble heart takes God's Word seriously and is sensitive to its message. In the Bible we read about king Josiah and how when he had the words of the book of God's Law read to him he tore his clothes which was what they did in those days as an outward sign of affliction. It was a public demonstration that he'd humbled himself before God and was trembling at the judgements which God's Word declared he and his people were deserving of. God valued, or esteemed - to use Isaiah's word - that reaction by king Josiah. For he went on to say to Josiah:

"because your heart was tender and you humbled yourself before the LORD when you heard what I spoke against this place and its inhabitants ... your eyes will not see all the evil which I will bring on this place" (2 Kings 22:19,20).

That's 'evil' in the sense of disaster, of course. Josiah, personally, would be spared God's judgements - and it was because of his attitude in taking God's Word to heart. The reason why God values humility in us is because it's a quality of his own nature. That may at first seem strange to us, for if we were to think of or imagine some human being in a position of great power and authority over others, I doubt if the adjective 'humble' would be the first one to come to mind as we thought about them. In our experience and observation perhaps greatness and power don't seem to be compatible with humility. In fact, society seems more and more to think of humility as a weakness - to the extent that employers might regularly put on training courses in self-assertiveness. To a point that can be helpful in business, but taken to extreme, in other areas, what the world says is: 'If you've got it, flaunt it'.

Naturally enough then, if we're conditioned by all that around us, it may seem strange to think of God as humble. After all, doesn't the Bible teach that God is sovereign? And all-powerful? Yes, it does! But it's only our wrong ideas that make us think this is incompatible with true, genuine humility. When that almighty God came into human experience in the person of Jesus Christ - miraculously combining in one person both divine and perfect human natures - he declared about himself: 'I am meek and lowly in heart'. And God is pleased when he sees a reflection of that in us.

In fact, the apostle Paul, when he was writing his Bible letter to the Church of God in Philippi, put it more strongly than that. He addressed the Christians in the Church of God in Philippi directly and commanded them:

> *"Do not merely look out for your own personal interests, but also for the interests of others. Have this attitude in yourselves which was also in Christ Jesus, who, although He existed in the form of God, did not regard equality with God a thing to be grasped, but emptied Himself, taking the form of a bond-servant, and being made in the likeness of men. And being found in appearance as a man, He humbled Himself by becoming obedient to the point of death, even death on a cross. Therefore also God highly exalted Him, and bestowed on Him the name which is above every name, that at the name of Jesus every knee should bow, of those who are in heaven, and on earth, and under the earth, and that every tongue should confess that Jesus Christ is Lord, to the glory of God the Father."* (Philippians 2:5-11)

Paul had been calling upon them to put the needs of others ahead of their own needs. Our fallen human nature tends to rebel at the unreasonableness of that. Is this pathetic weakness? Not a bit of it! Let's put aside these warped notions - the reality is we're talking here about true godliness: about acting towards others in the same way as God in Christ has acted towards us.

We pause to give thanks that the God of heaven, the God of eternity, is genuinely interested in us! And shown it to the extent he has done by coming to rescue us from our fallenness and sin and make possible our being re-created in his own image. These verses more than anywhere else in the Bible perhaps reveal the heart of God - lay it bare for us to see, and worship.

We need to be clear from Paul's words (which are God's words, of course) in Philippians chapter 2: God the Son did not become humble when he entered into humanity as the baby born as Jesus Christ in Bethlehem. We're explicitly told that while the Lord existed in the form of God - while from all eternity he possessed the divine nature - this same attitude of humility resided in him. It was this attitude that produced the action of his coming to earth, even his planned, scheduled arrival at the cross to offer his life in death as payment for our sins. The truth is: no one ever cared for us like Jesus.

Paul goes on to talk about his young co-worker, Timothy, who showed a Christ-like spirit in that he had a genuine concern for the welfare of the Church of God at Philippi. This is how Paul introduces Timothy to them:

> *"But I hope in the Lord Jesus to send Timothy to you shortly, so that I also may be encouraged when I learn of your condition. For I have no one else of kindred spirit who will genuinely be concerned for your welfare. For they all seek after their own interests, not those of Christ Jesus."* (Philippians 2:19-21)

"The interests of Jesus Christ" is an expression we can draw from this Philippians' letter. Paul was writing disappointingly of believers whose chief concern was their own interests, he says, not the interests of Jesus Christ. But, he tells us, Timothy was different. He had Christ's interests at heart. This was said to be demonstrated by his concern for the welfare of those in the church of God at Philippi (2:20-21). From this we can learn of the deep interest of Jesus Christ in churches of God as we find them biblically defined in New Testament times.

When, with a humble heart, we tremble at God's Word, would we not expect like Timothy to enter into the treasured interests of Jesus Christ in Churches of God?

CHAPTER 3: A GOD-FEARING HEART

———

We're imagining God to have a treasure box, and wondering what might be in it. I'm making a few suggestions and inviting you to check out the biblical support for each of them. Basically, what we're doing is trying to identify from the Bible the kind of heart God treasures. God speaks of something he treasures towards the close of the book of the prophet Malachi, right at the end of the Old Testament. By that time people were becoming a bit cynical. They were expressing their doubts as to whether serving God was all that it was cracked up to be. It was a case of the now all too familiar, 'What's in it for me?' mentality.

Malachi told the doubters then that even though there might be no apparent benefit in serving God right now, one day there would be shown to be great benefit. His message from God was:

> "On [that] day ... you shall again discern between the righteous and the wicked, between one who serves God and one who does not serve Him. For behold, the day is coming, burning like an oven and all the proud, yes, all who do wickedly will be stubble. And the day which is coming shall burn them up," says the LORD.

So what exactly would be the benefit of following God's way? It's as if God now turns to the other type of person among his people - to the God-fearing ones - and tells them. Of them we discover:

> *"Those who feared the LORD spoke to one another, and the LORD listened and heard them; so a book of remembrance was written before Him for those who fear the LORD and who meditate on His name. "They shall be Mine, "says the LORD of hosts, "On the day that I make them My jewels. And I will spare them as a man spares his own son who serves him."...*
>
> *To you who fear My name the Sun of Righteousness shall arise with healing in His wings; You shall trample the wicked, for they shall be ashes under the soles of your feet on the day that I do this, "says the LORD of hosts."*
> (Malachi 3:16-4:3 NKJV)

'A book of remembrance' - the king in the story of Esther had one of those (Esther 2:23). One night when he couldn't sleep he read it and discovered he hadn't rewarded a man who'd uncovered an attempt on his life. The king's determination to reward him reversed the fortunes of the arch-enemy of God's people in those days - as you can remind yourself by reading the book of Esther again. But it's not as if the God of eternity, the King of the Ages needs reminding. So, why a book of remembrance? Surely, it's God's way of accommodating to our way of thinking. The language of the book of Revelation agrees that one day - in the day of final judgement - books will be opened before God. God's righteous judgement will be seen to be fair, according to what everyone has done in this life - with those actions making absolutely clear as to whether we really trusted in God and his salvation or not.

Do you remember what God said to those who respected him and served him humbly and overcame their doubts and thought and spoke together about the things of God? I think it's lovely: *"They shall be Mine, "says the LORD of hosts, "On the day that I make them My jewels."* It's obvious enough, I think, that the expression 'my jewels' means a very special treasure. And that's certainly confirmed if we check up on the Bible word that's used here. It was something the owner shut up securely and kept it closely to himself as his prized possession.

Solomon used the word when he wrote in Ecclesiastes 2:8 about silver and gold and the peculiar - or special - treasures of kings. His father, David the king, used the same word to describe his special royal treasure which he was dedicating for the building of God's temple (1 Chronicles 29:3). Talk of diamonds in the rough! Can you imagine God - the Great King - making a wretch like me - and like you - into treasure for himself: his very own prized and unique treasure? It should thrill us to think of it!

More than that, it's exactly the word God used when he gave his people the Law through Moses and promised that if they obeyed him they would be a very special treasure to him. Three times in the book of Deuteronomy (7:6; 14:2; 26:18) God repeats that this is what he wanted his people to be to him - his own special treasure. In the time of the prophet Malachi, a thousand years later, it was only a small proportion of the people that were then living up to God's aspiration. But he really valued them for doing so! I don't think we could overestimate the value God places on a God-fearing heart.

By a God-fearing person, of course, we mean someone who has respect for God, someone whose lifestyle reverences God. The main way in which this will be seen will be in that person's attitude to the Word of God, the Bible. After all, it was if his people long ago obeyed his Word, that God said he'd then make them his treasured possession.

The New Testament makes it clear that God's still looking for the same thing. There's really a very close parallel between the language God used in Exodus chapter 19 and the things he says to us through the apostle Peter's writing in the New Testament. Let's refresh our memory of Exodus 19 first, God said: *"Now if you obey me fully and keep my covenant, then out of all nations you will be my treasured possession. Although the whole earth is mine, you will be for me a kingdom of priests and a holy nation."* (Exodus 19:5-6 NIV)

Now compare that with its New Testament equivalent, spoken to Christian believers in New Testament churches of God, spoken through Peter in his first letter, chapter two:

> *"But you are a chosen race, a royal priesthood, a holy nation, a people for God's own possession, that you may proclaim the excellencies of Him who has called you out of darkness into His marvelous light; for you once were*

not a people, but now you are the people of God; you had
not received mercy, but now you have received mercy."
(1 Peter 2:9-10)

In place of 'a people for God's own possession' another version (NKJV) says 'His own special people'. Both of these correspond to 'my treasured possession' which is the Old Testament wording. God-fearing Israelites long ago obeyed the Law and so were viewed by God as featuring among his treasured possession; and so today God-fearing believers who obey the biblical commands of the Christian Faith are assured of the same great blessing - being among God's treasures! The prophet Isaiah tells us 'the fear of the LORD is his treasure' (33:6). Isn't that wonderful!

CHAPTER 4: AN OBEDIENT HEART

———

Do you remember the description of my daughter's treasure box in the first chapter? Now what we're doing is imagining God to have a treasure box. And we're making a few suggestions as to what might be in it if that were the case - thinking in terms of the kind of heart that God treasures. So far, the candidates for the treasure box have been a worshipping heart, a humble heart and a God-fearing heart. I invite you to check out the biblical support for each of that list of suggestions. Next we're going to suggest that an obedient heart is another kind of heart God treasures. To help us see that, please consider with me an incident from the career of Israel's first king, King Saul. One day:

> *"Samuel said to Saul, "I am the one the LORD sent to anoint you king over his people Israel; so listen now to the message from the LORD. This is what the LORD Almighty says: I will punish the Amalekites for what they did to Israel when they waylaid them as they came up from Egypt. Now go, attack the Amalekites and totally destroy everything that belongs to them. Do not spare them; put to death men and women, children and infants, cattle and sheep, camels and donkeys."*

So Saul summoned the men and mustered them at Telaim - two hundred thousand foot soldiers and ten thousand men from Judah. Saul went to the city of Amalek and set an ambush in the ravine ... Then Saul attacked the Amalekites all the way from Havilah to Shur, to the east of Egypt He took Agag king of the Amalekites alive, and all his people he totally destroyed with the sword. But Saul and the army spared Agag and the best of the sheep and cattle, the fat calves and lambs - everything that was good. These they were unwilling to destroy completely, but everything that was despised and weak they totally destroyed.

Then the word of the LORD came to Samuel: "I am grieved that I have made Saul king, because he has turned away from me and has not carried out my instructions. Samuel was troubled, and he cried out to the LORD all that night. Early in the morning Samuel got up and went to meet Saul, but he was told, "Saul has gone to Carmel. There he has set up a monument in his own honour and has turned and gone on down to Gilgal."

When Samuel reached him, Saul said, 'The LORD bless you! I have carried out the LORD'S instructions." But Samuel said, "What then is this bleating of sheep in my ears? What is this lowing of cattle that I hear?" Saul answered, "The soldiers brought them from the

Amalekites; they spared the best of the sheep and cattle to sacrifice to the LORD your God, but we totally destroyed the rest."

"Stop!" Samuel said to Saul. "Let me tell you what the LORD said to me last night." "Tell me," Saul replied. Samuel said, "Although you were once small in your own eyes, did you not become the head of the tribes of Israel? The LORD anointed you king over Israel. And he sent you on a mission, saying, 'Go and completely destroy those wicked people, the Amalekites; make war on them until you have wiped them out.' Why did you not obey the LORD? Why did you pounce on the plunder and do evil in the eyes of the LORD?"

"But I did obey the LORD," Saul said. "I went on the mission the LORD assigned me. I completely destroyed the Amalekites and brought back Agag their king. The soldiers took sheep and cattle from the plunder, the best of what was devoted to God, in order to sacrifice them to the LORD your God at Gilgal."

But Samuel replied: "Does the LORD delight in burnt offerings and sacrifices as much as in obeying the voice of the LORD? To obey is better than sacrifice, and to heed is better than the fat of rams. For rebellion is like the sin of divination, and arrogance like the evil of idolatry. Because you have rejected the word of the LORD, he has rejected you as king." (1 Samuel 15:1-23 NIV)

Rejected! What a fearful sentence for a man who had been on a mission for the Lord. More than that, he felt sure it had been a successful mission in every area that mattered. How could anyone find fault with this brainwave of using some of the cattle for worshipping the LORD rather than unnecessarily killing them all? Whether it truly was the soldiers' initiative or not, Saul had at least adopted the idea, and authorized the action. But the end result is worshipping God, so surely that makes everything all right?

How wrong could Saul be! He soon learnt from Samuel - in uncompromising terms. The king who'd proudly been building himself a congratulatory monument was now confronted by the prophet who had spent the time humbly consulting God. The bottom line of Samuel's denunciation of Saul's actions was this: *'to obey is better than sacrifice'*. Saul's intention to offer sacrifices to God was at the expense of obeying God fully in terms of the Lord's carefully worded mission statement. Saul had been asked to wipe everything out and so not to retain any plunder - for whatever purpose. Good intentions, even the sincerest, cannot compensate or excuse disobedience.

The Lord has sent us on a mission too: *"Go therefore and make disciples of all the nations, baptizing them in the name of the Father and the Son and the Holy Spirit, teaching them to observe all that I commanded you; and to, I am with you always, even to the end of the age"* (Matthew 28:19-20). Saul for his part had not observed all that he'd been commanded to do, and the Lord held him accountable for that. Dare we presume his attitude will be any different in our case?

A lady was telling me the other day about a sales manager refusing to honour an offer coupon she'd cut from her newspaper and taken into the store. He'd actually taken a magnifying glass to show her in the small print - so small that it needed a magnifying glass to be legible it seems - to show her that the offer was invalid on the particular type of item she wanted to purchase. God doesn't do that to us. His commands were clear and bold to Saul - as are all his commands to us in the New Testament - but he <u>will</u> hold us to the precise terms of his commands. To presume this and that doesn't apply to us any more is to fail to respect God's Word, and so fail to honour God.

Through the apostle Paul, God signalled to Timothy that the standard of teaching given to the first generation of Christian believers to uphold was binding on the next and subsequent generations. Timothy was to obey the original pattern of Christian teaching as Paul had done without leaving any bits out. Paul made it so clear:

> *"Retain the standard of sound words which you have heard from me, in the faith and love which are in Christ Jesus. Guard, through the Holy Spirit who dwells in us, the treasure which has been entrusted to you."* (2 Timothy 1:13- 14)

And so there's our word 'treasure'. A reminder to us that God treasures our obedience. God prizes an obedient heart!

CHAPTER 5: A WISE UNDERSTANDING HEART

———

D o you have a treasure box? Perhaps you have a fire-proof box-file for important documents. Other things people keep safe are things that have sentimental value. If we were to imagine God having a treasure box, I wonder what would be in it? In this book we're checking out a few suggestions as to the kind of heart God treasures. King Solomon in the Old Testament illustrates another kind of heart, another quality that God prizes. It's easy to identify it from the charming story in which the Lord invites Solomon to ask for anything he wants. This is what happened:

> "At Gibeon the LORD appeared to Solomon during the night in a dream, and God said, "Ask for whatever you want me to give you." Solomon answered, "Now, O LORD my God, you have made your servant king in place of my father David. But I am only a little child and do not know how to carry out my duties ... So give your servant a discerning heart to govern your people and to distinguish between right and wrong. For who is able to govern this great people of yours?"

> The Lord was pleased that Solomon had asked for this. So God said to him, "Since you have asked for this and not for long life or wealth for yourself, nor have asked for the death of your enemies but for discernment in

administering justice, I will do what you have asked. I
will give you a wise and discerning heart, so that there
will never have been anyone like you, nor will there ever
be. Moreover, I will give you what you have not asked
for - both riches and honour - so that in your lifetime
you will have no equal among kings. And if you walk in
my ways and obey my statutes and commands as David
your father did, I will give you a long life." (1 Kings
3:5-14 NIV)

The pleasure God expressed when Solomon asked for a wise
and discerning heart shows to us how much God treasures
discernment. Solomon later wrote proverbs about wisdom being
more valuable than rubies and silver. In saying what he did he
was reflecting God's own set of values.

Solomon is described in the Bible as the man to whom God
appeared twice. I imagine these two appearances were among the
greatest highlights of his life. It seems natural to link them both
together. Following that first time when the Lord appeared to
Solomon, Solomon had acted wisely - especially in things to do
with the construction of the Jerusalem Temple. In fact, it was:

"When Solomon had finished building the temple of the
LORD and the royal palace, and had achieved all he
had desired to do, [that] the LORD appeared to him
a second time, as he had appeared to him at Gibeon.
The LORD said to him: "I have heard the prayer and
plea you have made before me; I have consecrated this

temple, which you have built, by putting my Name there for ever. My eyes and my heart will always be there." (1 Kings 9:1-3 NIV)

What prayer was God answering? Well, earlier Solomon had said:

"The LORD has kept the promise he made: I have succeeded David my father and now I sit on the throne of Israel, just as the LORD promised, and I have built the temple for the Name of the LORD, the God of Israel. I have provided a place there for the ark, in which is the covenant of the LORD that he made with our fathers when he brought them out of Egypt."

Then Solomon stood before the altar of the LORD in front of the whole assembly of Israel, spread out his hands towards heaven and said: "O LORD, God of Israel, there is no God like you in heaven above or on earth below - you who keep your covenant of love with your servants who continue wholeheartedly in your way. You have kept your promise to your servant David my father; with your mouth you have promised and with your hand you have fulfilled it - as it is today. Now LORD, God of Israel, keep for your servant David my father the promises you made to him when you said, 'You shall never fail to have a man to sit before me on the throne of Israel, if only your sons are careful in all they do to walk before me as you have done.

'And now, O God of Israel, let your word that you promised your servant David my father come true. But will God really dwell on earth? The heavens, even the highest heaven, cannot contain you. How much less this temple I have built! Yet give attention to your servant's prayer and his plea for mercy, O LORD my God. Hear the cry and the prayer that your servant is praying in your presence this day. May your eyes be open towards this temple night and day, this place of which you said, 'My Name shall be there, 'so that you will hear the prayer your servant prays towards this place ..."

I'm really struck by those words: *'My Name shall be there'.* In his prayer Solomon was quoting back God's own words. Concerning the splendid Temple Solomon had built for God at Jerusalem, God had promised: *'My Name shall be there'.*

Solomon's God-given discernment is shown by his grasp of this awesome reality that God's Name was identified with the place where the Temple was. He seemed to have been gripped by the wonder of that thought - and I've been gripped by it too just through reading about it again. Solomon's prayer displays his wonderful God-given wisdom because of its focus on the place God had chosen to establish his name for a dwelling - just as he'd promised to choose such a place back in the time of Moses (Deuteronomy 12:5). But what did this mean? What did it mean that God was going to place his name in a particular place? For God's Name to be in a place signified that his presence was there. It's also true in the New Testament that a person's name stood for the actual presence of that person. One place we see this is at the beginning of the Acts of the Apostles. After the disciples had seen Jesus ascend back into heaven:

> "... they returned to Jerusalem from the mount called Olivet, which is near Jerusalem, a Sabbath day's journey. And when they had entered, they went up into the upper room where they were staying: Peter, James, John, and Andrew; Philip and Thomas; Bartholomew and Matthew; James the son of Alphaeus and Simon the Zealot; and Judas the son of James. These all continued with one accord in prayer and supplication, with the women and Mary the mother of Jesus, and with His brothers. And in those days Peter stood up in the midst of the disciples (altogether the number of names was about a hundred and twenty)" (Acts 1:12-15 NKJV).

The first New Testament churches that were formed from these original disciples very soon afterwards were 'of God': they were actually called in the Bible churches of God. What's in a name, we ask? Plenty, if that name is God's Name! We, too, will be wise - and it will give God pleasure - if we discern that as far as our Christian testimony is concerned we, too, should put our names where God has put his own.

Did you love *The Visions of Zechariah*? Then you should read *Unlocking Hebrews* by Brian Johnston!

HEBREWS

BRIAN JOHNSTON

The letter to the Hebrews has been called "the forgotten letter of the New Testament". But, as Bible teacher and radio broadcaster Brian Johnston outlines in this little book, the letter contains a marvellous, divine revelation that is not found anywhere else in the Bible!The writer of the letter is concerned that new Jewish believers might be soon be walking away from their new-found faith and reverting back to Judaism. He passionately explains through a series of "warnings" exactly what they will be missing, the unique superiority of Jesus Christ, but also an amazing insight into the location of the collective worship of God, which remains unchanged 2,000 years later and gives incredible meaning to the Tabernacle service of the Old Testament!

Also by Brian Johnston

About the Bush: The Five Excuses of Moses
The Five Loves of God
Deepening Our Relationship With Christ
Really Good News For Today!
A Legacy of Kings - Israel's Chequered History
Minor Prophets: Major Issues!
The Tabernacle - God's House of Shadows
Tribes and Tribulations - Israel's Predicted Personalities
Once Saved, Always Saved - The Reality of Eternal Security
After God's Own Heart : The Life of David
Jesus: What Does the Bible Really Say?
God: His Glory, His Building, His Son
The Feasts of Jehovah in One Hour
Knowing God - Reflections on Psalm 23
Praying with Paul
Get Real ... Living Every Day as an Authentic Follower of
Christ
A Crisis of Identity
Double Vision: Hidden Meanings in the Prophecy of Isaiah
Samson: A Type of Christ
Great Spiritual Movements
Take Your Mark's Gospel
Total Conviction - 4 Things God Wants You To Be Fully
Convinced About
Esther: A Date With Destiny
Experiencing God in Ephesians
James - Epistle of Straw ?
The Supremacy of Christ
The Visions of Zechariah
Encounters at the Cross
Five Sacred Solos - The Truths That the Reformation Recovered

Kingdom of God: Past, Present or Future?
Overcoming Objections to Christian Faith
Stronger Than the Storm - The Last Words of Jesus
Fencepost Turtles - People Placed by God
Five Woman and a Baby - The Genealogy of Jesus
Pure Milk - Nurturing New Life in Jesus
Jesus: Son Over God's House
Salt and the Sacrifice of Christ
The Glory of God
The Way: Being a New Testament Disciple
Power Outage - Christianity Unplugged
Windows to Faith: Insights for the Inquisitive
Home Truths
60 Minutes to Raise the Dead

About the Author

Born and educated in Scotland, Brian worked as a government scientist until God called him into full-time Christian ministry on behalf of the Churches of God (www.churchesofgod.info). His voice has been heard on Search For Truth radio broadcasts for over 30 years (visit www.searchfortruth.podbean.com) during which time he has been an itinerant Bible teacher throughout the UK and Canada. His evangelical and missionary work outside the UK is primarily in Belgium and The Philippines. He is married to Rosemary, with a son and daughter.

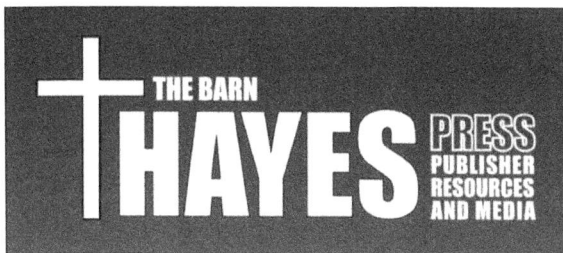

About the Publisher

Hayes Press (www.hayespress.org) is a registered charity in the United Kingdom, whose primary mission is to disseminate the Word of God, mainly through literature. It is one of the largest distributors of gospel tracts and leaflets in the United Kingdom, with over 100 titles and hundreds of thousands despatched annually. In addition to paperbacks and eBooks, Hayes Press also publishes Plus Eagles Wings, a fun and educational Bible magazine for children, and Golden Bells, a popular daily Bible reading calendar in wall or desk formats. Also available are over 100 Bibles in many different versions, shapes and sizes, Bible text posters and much more!

www.ingramcontent.com/pod-product-compliance
Lightning Source LLC
Chambersburg PA
CBHW021218020426
42331CB00003B/364